Invisible Guardians

Invisible Guardians

True Stories of Fateful Encounters

by

Jakob Streit

Illustrations by Christiane Lesch

Translated from the German by Nina Kuettel

AWSNA

Printed with support from the Waldorf Curriculum Fund

Published by:
The Association of Waldorf Schools
of North America
Publications Office
65–2 Fern Hill Road
Ghent, NY 12075

Title: *Invisible Guardians*
Author: Jakob Streit
Translator: Nine Kuettel
Editor: David Mitchell
Copy Editor and Proofreader: Ann Erwin
© 2011 by AWSNA
ISBN # 978-1-936367-17-7
First published by Verlag Freies Geistesleben, 1992
Original ISBN 3-7725-1145-5
Published with rights given by Jakob Streit and his estate

TABLE OF CONTENTS

PREFACE

The stories in this book are based on actual events. Some of them were told to me during conversations, and a few are taken from my own experiences. Still others came to me by way of letters that were written in answer to a survey. Only a portion of those were suited for the purpose of re-telling as a story. However, all the people who reported such experiences were consistent in their belief that a guiding force had intervened in their destiny.

Jakob Streit

The Fall

Years ago I was spending my summer vacation in lonely Fermeltal in the Swiss Alps. Every evening I observed smoke rising from the chimney of a remote chalet. I knew that good cheese was being made there from the herb-rich milk. One evening I wandered toward the chalet. The cows had been milked and were grazing on the dusky meadow. A young cowherd was just washing his milking utensils at a perpetually flowing water hydrant and trough in front of the chalet.

I went up to greet him. He cheerfully returned my greeting with a big smile that seemed to envelop his whole face. He was probably happy to see someone besides the elderly man who helped him with the cows. He invited me in for a cup of fresh milk. The other man was sitting in front of the fire, using a wooden stick to stir a large copper kettle filled with milk. It would become cheese.

The old man returned my greeting with a nod of his head but was not distracted from his work. By the time the two men learned that I was staying further down the valley in the house of the schoolmaster (mountain people like to know where people come from), the milk jug was on the table, and Res, the young man, drank along.

After a while, the elderly cowherd sat down beside me, and Res continued the stirring. I stayed by the fire with the others, as there was no other light in the room, until the fresh cheese was lifted out of the kettle with a cloth and pressed into a round wooden form. We had a good conversation in the smoky room by weak firelight.

When it was time to go, the older man said: "This evening was too short. Come see us again tomorrow night." And Res shook my hand with such strength I thought my bones might crack.

The following evening I was sitting with them again, and Res became talkative. He told us about something he had experienced up here ten years ago when he was still a young herd boy:

That summer I was helping to look after the cows on the Schwarzalp. When I was watching the cows, day in and day out, I would oftentimes look back in the valley at the dark cliffs of the Spitzhorn Alp. Among the cowherds it is said that wild vermouth grows there, a highly-prized herb for tea. The herb gatherers had already picked everything down below, but up above, higher in the cliffs, it could still be found. But the Spitzhorn is not without danger.

One day, as we were drinking our breakfast milk, my grandfather said to the cowherd: "I have a devil's yearning for some bitter tea made from wild vermouth, but it's too hard for me to climb the cliffs. What a pity!" Immediately, I thought: 'I could go up there secretly and return with the herbs. He would be so proud of me! And, a poor herdboy needs to hear some praise once in a while.'

One day that summer it was so hot that the cows, plagued by biting flies, crowded into the barn early in the afternoon. As soon as I finished tying them up, I went into the kitchen, quickly drank some cool milk, and started out toward the Spitzhorn. The cowherd always came around three o'clock in the afternoon to milk the cows, but I planned on being back before then. Over the rolling hills I went at a fast pace, and then a little more leisurely among the big rocks, upward from boulder to boulder. Soon the chalet was far below me.

When I reached the first slippery ridge of the cliff, I climbed onto the rocks. Yes, there they were, the vermouth plants with the little yellow blossoms! I feverishly picked the herbs and stuffed them into the leather satchel, all the while chewing on some of the bitter leaves. I even stuffed my pockets full. On all sides of me the cliffs descended steeply into the depths below. One time a rock was loosened under my foot, and I heard it thunder downward. I began the climb down the cliff. I noticed an especially splendid plant a little to the side. I wanted to take it with me. I slipped while trying to reach it and was about to fall on a sharp outcropping of rocks below. While I was teetering, I screamed: "Help me, God!" and desperately tried to jump a little to the side where there was a depression with smaller, rounded rocks at the bottom. Impact – rolling head-over-heels – hard blows to my head and bones – buzzing and flickering – trying to protect myself – scratches—thud!

Battered, I lay there on the pile of rocks. There was dust, sand, and blood in my mouth, nose, and eyes, and pain everywhere. After some rubbing, spitting, and sniffling, I tried to stand up. Oh, miracle, I could do it! Very carefully, almost mechanically, I climbed out of the shallow hole, and lay on the grass in the sun. A butterfly seesawed above my bloody hand and took a little nip of blood.

For a long time I sat by the mountain brook, washing my arms, my torn knees, my face, and my blood-encrusted hair. It slowly dawned on me that my intuitive leap onto the pile of rocks had saved my life. My skull would have shattered on the sharp cliff rocks. In my mind I heard my own desperate cry as if in an echo chamber: 'Help me, God!'

When I arrived back at the chalet, the cowherd was not there yet. I put the herbs in the haymow to dry. I put on my rain hat because my head was still bleeding. Since I had rolled up my sleeves on the cliffs, now I was able to cover my wounded arms with them. Fortunately, my leg bones had not been injured. I did not want the cowherd to know anything about my misadventure. When he arrived, I was hard at work, and I clamped my jaw shut tight to keep from wailing in pain. Every once in a while I forced myself to yodel a little as was my habit.

That night I spread a large handkerchief over my pillow so it would not get soiled with blood. For many nights I could sleep only on one side.

During the day, while I was watching the cows, I gratefully chewed on some of the wild vermouth. I wore long sleeves for a long time to cover my healing wounds. Now I look at the cliffs of the Spitzhorn Alp with very different eyes. Somehow, whenever I look upon them, I get a feeling of strength, courage, and confidence, even now, long after all my wounds have healed and once again I go bare-headed and with my sleeves rolled up.

On the Alp

One summer day the Wilde family drove into the mountains with their four children. They knew a place up there, close to a stream, at the edge of a pine forest. When they arrived, the parents unloaded lounge chairs and wool blankets from the car trunk and set up their resting place a short distance away. The children declared: "Lying around is boring. We're going to play over there by the water!"

After they had played for a little while, the oldest boy said: "Let's gather some wood for a bonfire for August First. (The First of August is the Swiss National Independence Day.) I have some matches, and then we can sing and yodel." It was no sooner said than done! They managed to make a very decent sized pile of wood. But because it had rained the night before, the wood was wet and it would not burn. What a disappointment!

The oldest boy said: "Dad has a can of gasoline in the car. Gas burns really well. If we spread a good amount on the wood it will burn great!"

Carl went to get the gas can, making sure he was not seen, and sprinkled some on the pile of wood. Still unnoticed, he took the can back to its place in the car. Now came the best part, lighting the bonfire! Five-year-old Thomas quickly stuffed a piece of wood into an open space in the wood pile. The match flamed. A fireball exploded. Little Thomas was set ablaze because his clothes were made from flammable synthetic material. Carl, the oldest, fell back in the grass from shock. The three-year-old youngest child ran screaming to his parents. Big sister Christina quickly rolled Thomas around in the damp grass to smother the fire of his burning clothes, and then she tore the smoldering clothing from his body. It was all very sudden and intense.

By the time their parents arrived at the scene everything was over. Only poor Thomas was lying there whimpering and naked in the grass with painful burns. Christina had singed her hair and burned her hands. But her little brother Thomas was saved. The cool water in the brook cooled the initial, intense pain. Thomas was wrapped in a blanket and driven to the hospital. It was necessary that he have an operation with skin grafting and a feeding tube. Christina got soothing bandages on her hands.

The next day while Christina and her mother were sitting together, her mother asked: "How did you know to roll your brother in the grass?" Christina replied: "I don't know. I just had to do it. I didn't think." Her mother hugged her and said: "The doctor said if there had been even a few more burns, the little one would have died. We could not have done anything for him. See, you were his guardian angel!" Christina said thoughtfully: "Yes, it's like he's a part of me now."

In the Helicopter

$\mathcal{A}$ lot of training is necessary to go from being a pilot of a simple, single-engine aircraft to being a confident captain of a helicopter. Carl did it. He became a flight instructor and taught many students. Among them was Paul, the youngest of his pupils. As an only son, Paul had a lot of trouble convincing his parents to allow him to start helicopter pilot training, but finally he did. He was far enough along in his training that sometimes he could fly by himself. One day there was a mishap. Carl described it as follows:

I said to Paul: "Tomorrow you can take the helicopter that has just been maintenanced by the mechanic and do a solo flight hour. I'm going up with Fred a little earlier. The key is in the office hanging on the board. Okay, I'll see you at ten o'clock!"

Not until I was at the airport with Fred and took out the key did I notice that I had thoughtlessly grabbed the wrong one and was holding the key to the helicopter that had just been overhauled. For a second I thought I should go back and exchange it, but then I thought: 'No need, Paul can just as easily take the other helicopter. He will take the key that is still hanging on the board.'

I got into the freshly overhauled machine with Fred. Everything had been cleaned and polished. I handed over the piloting to my pupil and sat next to him. When we had reached an altitude of 1800 feet, it happened: engine failure! Oil flowed into the fuel and a cloud of smoke shot out. The engine's power collapsed and we began to sink. Quick as a flash I took over the piloting. By auto-rotating the rotor blades I was able to stop the helicopter from descending in a twirling motion. Just before we hit the ground I put on the brakes. We were able to land on the shoulder of a highway. The quick maneuver was successful: no damage to the machine and no injuries to the passengers.

Soon we heard sirens from the fire department, police, and ambulance. They had nothing to do but shake hands and haul away the defective helicopter. If I had not mistakenly picked up the wrong key a half hour earlier, Paul, the young student pilot, would have certainly crashed to his death in that helicopter.

Looking back, I get a strange feeling when I think that in the moment of taking the key, consciousness was suspended for a second, because that is the only way the tragedy could have been prevented.

Rage in an Airplane

*A*n airplane pilot tells this story: It was summertime. One morning I was supposed to pilot a survey flight on a four-passenger airplane. At breakfast my two boys were pleading: "Dad, can't we fly with you today? It's such beautiful weather! Mom will come too." For some reason I didn't like the idea of turning this service flight into a family outing so I said: "No."

The reconnaissance flight took me way up over the clouds and my feet were freezing in my light summer shoes. A second solo flight was planned for an hour later. Should I call my wife and ask her to bring my heavy, high-top hiking boots? 'No,' I thought again. 'That would be a bother.' But a little while later I called her anyway, maybe because I just wanted to talk to her. She thought it was a little odd that I was asking for my heavy shoes, but she brought them to the airport and I changed into them right away.

After a short rest I started out on the second survey flight. So far, so good; I finished the task. I turned around and began preparations for landing. When I pushed the lever to release the landing gear, there was a loud cracking noise. I was holding the broken-off lever in my hand! My first reaction was: 'Oh, my gosh!' But then it became clear that it was useless to think the wheels could be lowered. There was no ejection seat. 'Stay calm. Don't get excited!' I ordered myself. I circled the landing field. Nothing could help. I radioed my serious situation to the control tower. After all suggestions for a remedy had been tried unsuccessfully, the order came to try a belly landing (no wheels). I knew this was more than dangerous. I circled a few more times to give them time to get a rescue team, a doctor, and an ambulance to the scene.

What I lived through in those moments is hard to describe. My life went before my inner eye in a panorama: my youth, my family, the two boys. Would their father be a cripple when they saw him again? Or would they lose him altogether? Frustration dimmed my clear thinking, and I stomped on the floor like crazy with both feet. There! A miracle! Evidently, I had pushed so hard against the stump of the lever with my wide, strong heels that the mechanism was pushed forward and the landing gear was released! I was able to make a normal landing and was saved.

This experience matured me. What was it inside of me that insisted on getting the hiking boots? Who loosed the fit of anger in me for which I had no explanation?

In the evening when I was telling my wife and the boys about my experience, she said something I had never heard her say before: "I always pray for you and trust that with God all things are possible." From then on my hiking boots were much more valuable to me.

The House Fire

There were several families who lived in a large apartment building. The Riedel family had three children. Gudrun was the oldest and in kindergarten. Florian had just turned three, and the youngest was still a baby. Her name was Brigitte, and she not only slept through the night but also half the next day.

One evening when the children were already in bed the telephone rang. Mrs. Riedel answered and after a few seconds said to her husband: "We should pick up the potatoes and vegetables from the Millers. They got them fresh from the farm today. Would you drive me over there quickly? The children are sound asleep. We'll leave a light on and be back very soon." So, the Riedels drove to their friends' house in town. After they had loaded everything in the car, Mrs. Miller invited them in: "Come inside and have a cup of coffee. It's already made." Mrs. Riedel said: "But only for a minute. The children are alone at home." But when adults sit down to coffee, then there is conversation, and so the visit lasted longer than they had intended.

Back at the Riedel house Florian was awake. He saw the light in the hallway through the door crack. He got up and looked for Father and Mother. He did not find them. But in the kitchen by the gas range, he did find a box of matches that was normally always put away. Back in his bedroom he sat down on the rug. He opened the little box and rubbed the brown match on the side like he had seen his mother do when she lit the gas stove. The little match flamed up and burned, bright and cheerful. When he blew it out there was a nice little plume of smoke. When he threw a little burning match in the air, there was an arc of light, and then it fell on the rug. There were a few pieces of paper lying about with drawings Gudrun had made. Suddenly they began to burn, and the rug with them. Florian took his little teddy bear and used it to hit at the fire. The flames became smaller but now the teddy bear was on fire. All at once Florian was really frightened. He woke up his big sister. She took her pillow and tried to put out the flames. But now the pillow was burning, and a window curtain also caught fire. Baby Brigitte was asleep in her crib and did not notice anything of all the goings on.

Still in their pajamas, the two hurried down one floor to a neighbor lady. After she had finally opened the door and heard what it was about she ran with the children back upstairs. Smoke came toward her from the open apartment door, and there were flames shooting out of the children's room. She quickly called the fire department. A fire station was very close by. They were soon there and able to put out the fire. The children's room was completely gutted: the beds, the toys, the closet, the ceiling light—everything was burned up. But, the miracle! The firemen could not believe their eyes. The crib with little sleeping Brigitte was standing a little to the side in the burnt-out room, completely unharmed! There was not even any soot on it. Not a hair on the child's head was burned, and she did not have any smoke inhalation. She slept on peacefully, even when the firemen moved the crib into the living room.

A car drove up. The parents were home. They walked into the ruined apartment to find their three children alive!

THE INTERRUPTED SWIM

The Maurer family was lucky enough to live together with a very loving grandmother. Every evening she told little George fairytales. He could not get enough of them. Again and again she had to tell the story of *Iron Hans*. When George was all grown up he told the following story from his childhood:

One Sunday when it was especially nice weather, I talked my parents into driving us to a nearby river where I could spend the day swimming. My grandmother declared: "I'm going to stay home and brew myself a good cup of coffee." So, the three of us went on our way. My parents made themselves comfortable in camping chairs. I swam and dived in the river and enjoyed the warm water.

Just as I was making my way back to my parents, I stepped on a devilishly sharp piece of glass sticking out of the gravel. It made a deep and painful cut. It bled profusely. A handkerchief was quickly wrapped around it, and my parents drove me back to the house to get a proper bandage.

As my father opened the front door we could smell gas. Father hurried into the kitchen, shut off the gas burner, and opened the window. Grandmother had wanted to warm some milk for her coffee. The milk boiled over and put out the gas flames. The whole house was full of gas. Grandmother was lying on the couch in the living room in a deep sleep. She could hardly be wakened. This is what had happened: As soon as she put the milk on the stove, she went to rest on the couch for just a minute, but she fell asleep. Father called the doctor. He diagnosed a light case of carbon monoxide poisoning.

If we had not returned home so soon because of my accident with the glass shard, we would have found our dear grandmother dead. And then I got the strangest feeling: With just a little bit of pain, I had been able to save my grandmother's life! She told me the story of *Iron Hans* many, many more times.

The Invisible Hand

$\mathcal{A}$ woman mountain climber tells this story: I made a trip to the mountains with my friend Hans. We always found it very nice to hike in the mountains together. One time we came upon a mountain lake. The water was shimmering blue-green in the sunlight. On one side of the small lake were some cliffs that were calling to Hans to climb them. He said: "I want to hike around the whole lake. Are you coming?" I hesitated and replied: "If those huge boulders weren't there I'd come." Hans laughed at me: "Are you scared of a few big rocks?" and he started out.

After a little while, after Hans had disappeared behind the bushes and rocks, I decided that I would show a little courage and follow after my friend. While I was climbing among the big boulders, all of a sudden I lost my balance and started to fall backwards where there was an outcropping of very sharp rocks. Like lightning, I was stabbed with the thought: 'You're going to break your back!' Then from behind I felt something that seemed like an invisible hand pushing me back upright. A shiver went through my whole body. I stood there among the rocks, unable to move. I did not climb further to find my friend. I was overcome with a feeling of deep happiness, an indescribable sense of gratitude. I felt like shouting for joy. I sat down on the stony ground. A short while later I walked slowly back to the meadow by the lake. A long while later my friend returned but it was impossible for me to tell him the story. He would have laughed at me.

Many years later, after we were long married, I told Hans about my experience on my birthday. I could do it now. We had grown to trust one another through many trials over the years. "Yes," he said slowly and earnestly, "That was your guardian angel."

The Deceased Sister

John had trained to be a stone mason. He had long held the desire to work in foreign countries. He also made a valiant effort to learn English so that he could communicate just about anywhere in the world. Finally, he found a job with a European company and he was employed at a construction site in Africa. He had often noticed how different the people there were than in Europe. John tells this story of one of his strange experiences:

I became friends with Mubu, a young, black African man. He took me to meet his family who were very gracious and friendly to me. At work, regulations required that everyone wear a safety helmet. That was such a bother for me in the intense heat so I always worked without this protection.

One evening I was visiting Mubu and his family. His sister Naima said to me: "You never told us that you had a sister who died as a child." I was astounded at her words and replied: "No, I never have. But how do you know?" Naima looked at me a little strangely with her big, dark eyes: "Your dead sister came to me and she is asking you, for her sake, to please wear a helmet at work tomorrow. Will you do it?" My first thought was: "What kind of nonsense is she talking?' But I replied: "The helmet bothers me while I'm working. I don't want to wear it." To my surprise Mubu cut in on the conversation: "My dear friend, what my sister sees and hears is always true. Please, wear it tomorrow. I will also wear my helmet."

At last the two brought me to the point that I agreed, and the next morning I wore the helmet. I was working underneath a crane when suddenly a large screw from high above me fell from it and landed squarely on my helmet. If I had not been wearing it, the heavy piece of iron would have broken my skull. As it was, I came away with just a very bad headache. The helmet had protected me from certain death. But I knew that my sister, who had died too soon, was alive! Yes, from the other side, she had saved my life.

At the Pharmacy

Bruno lived alone with his mother in a large city. She went to work every day but was always home around five o'clock in the evening. She helped Bruno with his homework or she read him a story. His mother read so beautifully. Then she would cook dinner and Bruno would set the table. They had it very nice together.

One day Bruno's mother became very sick. In spite of the fever she still went to work. When she returned at five o'clock she was hardly able to climb the stairs. She staggered into the house and went right to bed. She called her doctor and he promised to stop by later in the evening. Bruno made tea for his mother, warmed some milk for himself, and sat quietly until the doorbell rang. The doctor's face was serious and he said: "My good woman, you have to go to the hospital!" Mother pointed to her boy and said: "We're alone here. We haven't been in the city very long. I don't know anyone who could take care of my son. I have to stay at home. He looks after me very well." The doctor answered: "I understand! But then the boy must go immediately to the pharmacy and pick up the medicine I am prescribing." To Bruno he said: "You know where the City Hall is? On the street behind it is Swan's Pharmacy. All the businesses are already closed. You will have to use the night bell to call the pharmacist." He explained to Bruno the shortest route to the pharmacy and promised to return the next day.

At ten years old Bruno was a capable and clever boy. He found the pharmacy even though it was already dark outside and snowing. But the pharmacist had gone out with his wife to the theater. He had asked his young apprentice to be on call that night on the slim chance that someone would come. The apprentice lived on the top floor of the shop and was lying in bed reading a very interesting book. When the bell rang he was a little irritated at the disturbance, but he went downstairs right away. He took the prescription from the boy and left him standing in the hallway, saying: "I'll be right back with this." After a very short time he was back with a small box of tablets and a little bottle of liquid. Bruno gave him the money from his mother's coin purse, and as fast as his feet would carry him, he hurried away so that his mother would be well again soon.

When the apprentice went to put the medicine bottle he had used back in its place, he noticed that he had filled the prescription from the wrong bottle and the one he had used contained a very poisonous substance. A wave of shock went through his whole body. He ran outside looking for the boy. He had not asked for his address. He could see the boy's footprints in the snow leading away from the door. But after just a few meters, all the other footprints obscured those he was following. He aimlessly ran down other streets, but it was no use. He was not able to stop the tragedy. Completely devastated, he turned and went back to the pharmacy. Desperately, he threw himself upon his bed. There was no way he could read. He stammered out words, half praying.

Suddenly the night bell rang again. The boy stood in front of the door crying and stuttering: "I slipped and fell. The bottle got broken. Please give me the medicine again. I will be very careful next time."

The boy did not understand why the apprentice was hugging him and patting him on the back. Soon the second bottle of medicine was ready. Bruno was looking in the coin purse to see if there was still money in there. The apprentice refused the money and said: "I will give it to you. It will help your mother! No, it doesn't cost anything."

A few days later his mother was recuperated. Only one person knew that a guardian angel had had something to do with it!

The Fencepost

The Michael family had rented a tiny mountain cabin in Switzerland for the New Year festivities where they could ski. Magdalena, who was four, was still too young to go skiing. But she jumped and cheered whenever her older brother came swooshing down a hill. The parents wanted to go to a farm with the two children where they could get some milk before evening. All four of them tramped through the steep snow-covered landscape. It was more tiresome going through the deep snow pulling a sled. What happened next was told to me by the mother:

While we were walking Magdalena was observing how her big brother would loosen a piece of frozen snow with his boot and watch it barrel down the hill and over the cliff. Suddenly Magdalena said: "I can also slide down!"

No sooner said than done. Very quickly she sat down on the sled and started sliding down the steep slope. Everything happened so fast. She swished and rolled and disappeared from our view. We knew that further down were dangerous cliffs, and we were scared to death. From above it was impossible to see where the cliff ended and how far down it was to the bottom. We heard Magdalena scream loudly. My husband and I ran downhill with our son right behind.

Our child had been caught on a short, old fence post. Anywhere to the right or left of it and she would have fallen over the cliff. A single post, apparently useless, peeked out a little above the snow. Probably the cowherd had not had time to clear away this last post in the autumn, or maybe he just forgot it. It had saved our Magdalena's life. Besides a few scrapes she was not injured. When we looked at the little girl's sled tracks we could see that she had made a gentle curve that brought her exactly to the post. We thanked the guardian angel who had directed

her downward slide so wisely, and we hugged our darling little girl who
was returned to us.

Tying the Shoes

$\mathcal{A}$ teacher reported: My class and I spent some beautiful winter days in a hut high up on the alp. On the last day when everything had been cleaned and put back in order, we headed down to the valley. There was snow clear down to the village, but once on the street that led down a narrow valley, we had to remove our skis and carry them on our shoulders. So that I could maintain control over my class I ordered: "I will lead at the front and no one is to hurry ahead of me!" I chose one brave lad to bring up the rear and said: "You watch that nobody stays behind. You and I should always be able to see one another."

We were descending lower and lower into the valley. To the left was a mountain forest on a steep slope with high cliffs overhanging. To the right, below the winding road, was a ravine with a mountain stream at the bottom. The boys and girls at the front were crowding up close to me because I would tell them funny stories or joke around with them. Suddenly I stopped and in a commanding tone said: "Stop! I have to tie my shoe!" The column jerked to a halt. In the same instant a hundred-pound boulder slammed down on the pavement a few meters in front of us and thundered down the ravine in a thousand pieces. If we had walked any further the boulder would have smashed us.

I had bent over to tie my shoe—but it was not untied! We stood there a moment as if paralyzed. Nobody said a word. Everyone looked at me. I could only whisper: "Thank God we came to a halt!" Slowly we got moving again.

The next day at school a boy came up to me and asked: "Teacher, how did you know about stopping yesterday?" I could only reply: "It must have been a guardian angel giving me a lightning fast command. They are often very quick!"

The Avalanche

$\mathcal{A}$ skier told about this experience: We were four good school friends on our way for a ski tour. Rudy, the only son of a poor widow, would not have been able to come with us if we had not all pitched in to buy his ski pass. He was always so cheerful and happy and we just could not leave him out. It was a beautiful day with a bit of a warm wind. On this tour we were staying far away from the lifts and the slopes. It was a climbing ski tour! The high altitude and powerful panoramic view were payment enough for all the effort.

Around four o'clock in the afternoon, having had our fill of beautiful experiences, we decided to start skiing back down to the valley. We always stayed within viewing distance of one another. From time to time we would stop to admire the gorgeous winter landscape. All at once, while we were standing together, we heard a thundering noise from further up the mountain. With a cry of: "Avalanche!" we scattered in all directions. When it was all over we looked around us in horror. Where was Rudy?! He was nowhere in sight. We went back to the path of the avalanche. Yes, he had skied in the wrong direction. We used our poles to jab everywhere into the avalanche snow. It was impossible to find our friend. Frustration overtook us. We were wildly and indiscriminately scratching and digging around in the snow. It was no use trying to find a person in this mass of white.

Suddenly we could see there was a skier with a dog high above us. We screamed and waved. He started on a course toward us. The unexpected helper was a soldier from an avalanche troop and had all the necessary equipment with him, including a small shovel. When he heard about our buried friend, he called his dog and said: "Search, Barry, search!" The dog ran over the avalanche snow back and forth a few times, sniffing like crazy. Very near the edge of the avalanche he began to scratch and dig.

We found Rudy really not so very deep in the snow, motionless, with his face on his arms. Was he still alive? Our helper commanded: "Two of you should go to that hut up there and bring back the big Canadian sled. We have to get him to the valley quickly!" And then the avalanche soldier worked for nearly a half hour to resuscitate Rudy. He was successful. As we were loading Rudy onto the sled, he was breathing and opened his eyes. He could not speak but he smiled before closing his eyes again.

Our helper expertly guided the sled down to the valley. Once down, he organized a car for us. Rudy was already able to stand and could get into the car by himself. After this terrifying fright, how unforgettably happy we were to return a living son to his mother.

I have often asked myself how it came to be that a helper and a dog appeared at precisely that moment and within calling distance.

THE BITING DOG

*I*n rural areas a minister often travels to lonesome farms to visit the sick and injured and comfort them. Only there is one problem: Sometimes a farm is guarded by an unfriendly dog, happy to attack strangers.

Reverend Huber knew, as he approached the Hubelbauren farm where the farmer's wife had taken ill, that a big, alert dog lived there. As a precaution he had brought along his walking stick and thought in all seriousness that he could defend himself with it if need be.

The farm stood there, silent. It was peaceful all around. The farmer was busy in the barn and the dog was not on the chain. As soon as the dog sensed the stranger coming closer, he darted out, bared his teeth, and barked ferociously. Reverend Huber stood still, his stick at the ready. But this powerful dog could bowl him over with one jump and it would be with him as it was with all those salesmen the dog had taken a dislike to and put in hospital.

Then something strange happened. The dog came to a halt about twenty feet in front of him, began shaking, bowed his head to the ground, and put his nose on his outstretched front paw. He even began whining and howling softly. Then suddenly he got up and trotted toward the farmhouse with his tail between his legs. The reverend walked behind him.

When the farmer heard the frantic barking, he had come out of the barn and seen his dog running toward two visitors. His shouts did not reach the ears of the loudly barking hound. He put his pitchfork aside in order to go meet the two men. But then he noticed that the dog was lying down submissively in front of the two visitors. 'Thank God!' he thought as the unfortunate salesmen went through his mind. 'The dog left them alone.' The homeward bound dog made a wide berth around the farmer and soon disappeared inside his doghouse. The farmer went on to welcome the minister. After he had greeted him, he asked: "Reverend, where has your companion disappeared to?" The minister replied in surprise: "I came alone. Nobody is with me. Your dog brought me out in a sweat!" But the farmer insisted: "Reverend, I could swear there was another person with you, a little taller than yourself."

The idea arose in Reverend Huber's mind that a protective presence must have stood by him. That would also explain the strange behavior of the dog. Was that perhaps the answer to his prayer for Divine protection when he saw the vicious dog racing toward him?

THE COMPANIONS

*F*lorian was a young gardener who took care of the garden and grounds of a hotel. He became friends with Julia who also worked at the hotel. A few days earlier a rich, important gentleman had arrived as a guest at the hotel and tried to win over the pretty Julia to be his girlfriend. But she rejected him and remained loyal to her gardener beau.

The lane up to the hotel was lined on both sides with old trees: an exquisite avenue. It led to a small village nearby. One evening Florian said to Julia: "Tonight I will be meeting a friend in the village. I will certainly not be back before midnight. I hope you will have a pleasant evening." The gentleman guest was sitting on the hotel terrace and overheard this conversation. His jealousy of the gardener addled his thoughts. He always carried a revolver in his luggage, and he thought: 'I could show that guy a thing or two in the avenue, a shot in the leg or something. I'm leaving tomorrow anyway. The hotel bill is paid.'

After the fine gentleman had downed a few whiskeys in the bar and dozed in front of the television, he left the bar about an hour before midnight. He got the gun from his room. Then he went to the avenue, further and further away from the hotel so that the shot could not be heard from there. He hid behind a wide tree trunk, stared at the ground, and waited. He had not waited long when he heard footsteps coming closer. In the weak moonlight he could see his rival coming. He recognized him by his gardener's hat. But what was this? There was someone walking on either side of him, and there was not one word exchanged between the three of them. The drawn weapon sank to his side. A wave of dizziness gripped him and he had to steady himself against the tree trunk. The three men disappeared up the avenue.

Back at the hotel the frustrated would-be shooter crawled to his room and fell into a leaden sleep. Oddly, the next morning when Julia was serving him breakfast in her usual friendly manner, a feeling of deep shame overcame him. Suddenly she did not interest him anymore. But he felt compelled to tell her how he had tried to ambush her friend last night. He kept silent about the revolver, saying only that he did not attack because her friend was with two other people walking home last night. This experience had freed him from his dark thoughts. "How stupid of me!" he said. He asked her forgiveness for being such a plague to them both. A surprised Julia shook his hand in farewell. Soon after, a white Mercedes drove away from the hotel.

After the guest had gone, Julia asked Florian who the two people were who accompanied him home last night. He could only assure her that he had returned home completely alone. Then Julia told him what the noble gentleman had confessed. "Florian, you should know that he had a revolver in his nightstand. The maid told me. I fear he had it with him last night." They were both certain that Florian's 'companions' had prevented a tragic event for him and the imprudent guest.

FELLING TREES

$\mathcal{D}$aniel's mother looked at her son, a little tyke of barely six years, with a little reluctance. He insisted in a strong voice: "Yes, Mother, I *want* to go to school in the spring; then I will finally have vacation, too! Father should go and sign me up."

"But Daniel, we've already told you so many times that you are too young. Only those children who are six years old by the New Year may go to school in the spring. That is how it is here!"

But Daniel did not give up: "Just because of a few days I'm too young, but Hans can go and he can't draw like me, or play the recorder like me, or count to a hundred."

As the two were having this conversation, the father walked in. He was a teacher and thought it would actually be very nice to walk with his little boy to the village school in the spring. Daniel stood before his father. Tears were very near, but he pressed on: "Father, please let me go to school this spring!" And then the tears flowed. He wrapped his arms around his mother and cried and cried. A little stunned, Mother looked at her husband. But Father just smiled: "Now, Daniel, if you absolutely want to go to school, I will talk with the school administrator and the teachers. You are really only a few days short. But if the answer is no, then you must stop harping on it." Daniel let go of his mother and was soon sitting on Father's arm and happily hugging his neck. Later, when they were alone, the father said to his wife: "Daniel is a very mature child. He draws wonderfully, has learned the alphabet by himself, and is very interested in everything in nature. He's ready for school. He might even become a leader in his class."

It happened as it had to happen. Daniel could start school in the spring. His radiant being did the whole class good. After just hearing a song, he could sing it with a full voice. His head was full of poems and verses that he cheerfully recited. His fellow pupils were amazed by his colorful drawings that shone above all the rest.

In the summer Daniel went with his family on vacation to the mountains. One morning his mother had a dream that Daniel would die a few days before her birthday. "Dreams are nothing but bubbles and foam," said her husband to whom she had told her disturbing dream. The holiday was over and life went on.

Autumn came. In the village forest there was something going on with the forester and his apprentices. Someone was making a documentary film about felling trees. Two school children were supposed to bring a basket of refreshments to the workers. The forester went personally to the school and chose the children: the lively Daniel and the curly-haired Sylvia.

In the forest they were cutting down an old beech tree, and the saws were rat-a-tat-tatting. Everything was professionally organized. The forester stood to one side of the place where the tree was expected to fall. He held the hands of both children. But what they did not realize is that the inside of the tree trunk was pretty hollow and so it fell in the wrong direction. As the tree was crackling, ready to fall, Daniel tore his hand away from the forester, ran a few steps, and was hit in the neck by a tree branch. He lay motionless on the ground underneath it. The branch was removed and the forester took the boy in his arms. He was dead.

Daniel's father was the first to hear the news. He was trying to think of a way to break it gently to his wife when she abruptly asked: "What happened to Daniel?" The forgotten dream suddenly appeared in her mind, and it was exactly eight days until her birthday.

Later, the parents often asked themselves: What was it that made Daniel want to go to school so badly? Why this class where the forester was looking for two children to help? Why was Daniel chosen? Why did he break away from the forester and run under the falling tree?' Somehow, the dream comforted his mother: "It was determined to be through God's wisdom." One thing led to another. Yes, it had to be so! The guardian angel became an angel of death to accompany a fulfilled, radiant child's life into death and on to new paths and new tasks that are hidden from us.

At the Rock Quarry

Work at a rock quarry is very hard. From there we get gravel for building roads and flagstones for building houses. Producing gravel requires big, powerful rock-crushing machines. In winter especially, working outside with the trucks and the machines is made more difficult by the cold weather. The workers really look forward to a rest for the Christmas holiday. A worker in just such a rock quarry tells this story:

It was getting close to Christmas. There was no snow and the work at the quarry was going full speed. I was eagerly anticipating the holiday with my family, and also the Christmas bonus in my paycheck. That evening I was going with my wife to buy Christmas presents for the children, but the day's work still had to be done before we got off early. In the quarry there was a big metal slide where the trucks would dump the broken rock. It would then slide a long way down to be crushed in a machine. To the side and above this slide I had to put up a ladder in order to change out a defective neon light. All at once the ladder I was standing on began to tip. I held on tight to the top of the ladder, but it swung toward the opening of the slide and I fell inside. I rolled like a stone down into ruin. Almost at the bottom I was able to stop myself, but I knew that in the next few minutes another truck would come and dump a load of rock down the slide. And that would be the end of me. I screamed even though I knew it was useless with the machines making so much noise. If I couldn't hold on or if the rocks soon came sliding down, I would be killed by the rock crusher. I felt that my right leg had been hurt. In the first pain of the realization I screamed: "Christmas! Christmas!"

But what was that? The rock crusher was running slower and suddenly it came to a standstill. No more rocks were coming from above. *Now scream as loud as you can!* And I screamed! This time the

40

other workers could hear me. They were able to get me free. My foot was broken, but the worst had been avoided. I found out from my coworkers why the rock crusher had suddenly stopped. While dumping some rock from a truck into the slide, one rock had hit the ladder that had fallen at the mouth of the slide and sent it flying. It landed squarely on the electrical box. The electricity went out and the machine stopped. No more rocks were dumped. I was saved. It didn't occur to me for days just how precisely it had all happened.

I sat under the Christmas tree with my stiff cast. My wife and children told me in more detail how strangely and quickly the chain of events had taken place. Little Gertrude said: "Right, Father, the Christmas Angel saved you so we could have you back with us!"

Twenty Cents Lost

*T*his is the story about something that happened to a young man when he was only five years old:

Unfortunately our mother had been really sick for a while. My father's pay was just enough for the doctor and medicine, but he could not afford to send my mother for a much-needed treatment at a convalescent facility. So money was really tight. One day my father gave me twenty cents and sent me across the street to buy a box of matches. Just as I was down there, a helicopter flew overhead, rather low. I looked up and gawked, walked a little way and gawked some more.

When I got to the store I realized that the coin was not in my hand. I was very upset. My father would be angry with me. My aunt lived nearby; she would help me. While I was hurrying over there, always searching on the ground, I discovered a brown briefcase. Curious five-year-old that I was, I sat down immediately between the streetcar tracks to inspect my find. The streetcar rang its bell, but I didn't hear anything as I pulled out red and brown papers from the leather case. I had no idea they were five-hundred and thousand franc notes.

The streetcar driver had to stop. He angrily got out so he could chase me away from the tracks. But what he saw left him wide-eyed and speechless. He gathered up all the money bills that were lying around me and stuffed them back into the briefcase. Other people got out of the streetcar and formed a curious ring around us. I started to cry. The driver picked me up and asked me where I lived. He probably thought I had taken the briefcase from home to play with it. He turned me over to another gentleman who was a stranger to us both, and that man took me home. He explained to my father what had happened. Then they counted the money together at the table. It totaled $15,000!

The briefcase owner's address was found inside. He owned an embroidery factory in the city. Since we had no telephone, the man who brought me home said: "I will call him right away. He can come here to pick up the money. According to the law your boy is entitled to $500 as a finder's fee." He waved goodbye.

My father finally asked about the matches. I confessed that I had lost the twenty cents and while looking for it I had found this brown thing. I really had no idea how much money that was. My father very lovingly said: "Whoever finds $15,000 is allowed to lose twenty cents."

A little while later the doorbell rang. A very well-dressed gentleman entered our poor abode. Everything was in order with the briefcase. He was very friendly with Father and Mother. He even asked about her illness. Before he left he laid $2,500 on the table as a finder's fee, and wished Mother a good recovery.

The money allowed my mother to undergo a thorough cure at a convalescent clinic. She came back so well recovered that we had her with us for many more years. The doctor said that without that time in the clinic, she probably would not have lived another year.

Courageous Act

*H*ere's what happened to little Ursula one First of August (Swiss Independence Day): As a school girl I spent every summer vacation with my aunt and uncle in Bergdorf. They lived in a big, beautiful chalet that had a barn built onto the side of it. I always especially enjoyed the First of August holiday. Bonfires shone from the tops of many mountains to celebrate the day. Music with trumpets and kettle drums was played in the village square. There was yodeling and dancing. So I looked forward to this summer day for many days ahead of time.

Wouldn't you know it? Just before this festival I became ill with a high fever. That was like a bad hailstorm on my child's sensibilities. Although I was put right to bed, the fever did not subside. So on the night of the celebration, I had to stay home alone in the quiet house. My aunt and uncle were working at a booth for one of the village clubs. It was a small consolation for me that they pushed my bed up to the window so that I could at least see some of the bonfires. Once in a while I would see some fireworks and hear their boom, but the quietly glowing fires on the Alps were nicer.

All at once a rocket that had gone awry shot in a straight line toward our house and crashed into the barn wall. It was still burning brightly when it fell. Suddenly it occurred to me that there was a pile of hay stored under the roof overhang. I was gripped with terrible fear. I jumped out of bed and hurried out of the house in my nightgown. Yes, the haystack under the eaves had already caught fire! Little flames were already lapping their way toward the wooden wall. Nobody heard my screams. I do not really know what came over me. I ran to the smoking, burning hay, grabbed a piece of canvas that was lying there, and began to beat the jumping flames to smother them. I paid no attention when my naked feet stepped on a glowing coal. I just beat at the fire and beat

at it until the last little spark was gone. Only then did I stop to think. From the distance I could hear dance music. I limped back to bed, my whole body shaking.

About an hour later my aunt and uncle came home. I was not asleep and I told them everything that had happened. They grabbed a lantern and went to have a look. They returned with pale faces and hugged me. Even my uncle had tears in his eyes. As my aunt was putting oil on my feet and bandaging the burns, she said: "Dearest Ursula, you were our guardian angel!" But I replied: "I think it must have been an angel that gave me the strength and courage!"

The next day I was well. The sweating I did while beating the fire had driven out the fever.

In a Foreign Country

Rolf was making an apprenticeship as a mechanic and considered: 'When I graduate I'm going to travel the whole world. When I'm twenty I'll get the payment from my childhood life insurance policy.' Rolf had been interested in Mexico for a long time, for the strange pyramids, and he had heard there were still Indians living there. He learned a few Spanish words from a dictionary. When the apprenticeship was complete and the insurance money received, the flight could be booked at a travel agency. Rolf tells the story of what he experienced in Mexico:

I flew to Mexico on a round trip ticket. When I arrived I still had 250 marks to live on. But I wanted to stay as long as possible. For three weeks everything went great. I paid for the inexpensive bed and breakfast and learned Spanish. Soon my cash money was almost gone. I stood on the street with my remaining fifteen marks. I found a very cheap, unfurnished room where I could stow my suitcase and sleep on a blanket on the floor. I ate bananas, only forty cents a kilo. That lasted for three days. I suffered terribly from hunger. There was only one thing I had enough of—time to go for walks. One day I meandered back and forth through Mexico City. Around midday I saw a taco stand in a populated city square advertising three tacos for fifty centavos. At that time it would have been about twenty pfennig. Tacos are hot corn tortillas filled with meat and beans and topped with hot sauce. Such an opportunity! My stomach growled powerfully. Deciding quickly, I bought the much needed food. I held the warm tacos in my hand for a moment and just took in their lovely perfume. I had not even noticed that beside me there were two boys in a fight. Just as I was about to take my first bite of the taco, one of the fighters crashed heavily into me, knocking my tacos to the ground and trampling them underfoot. I could have cried. Nothing but bananas for three days and then finally some real food! I did not want to buy again, so the hunger remained, even after I ate another banana.

Two days later I read in the newspaper in thick black headlines: *Xochimilico – Spoiled Meat Taken from Garbage and Used to Make Tacos. Many Customers – Poor People – in Hospital with Serious Food Poisoning.* I asked about the exact address of the taco stand in the newspaper. It was the same one where I had been so drastically relieved of my lunch. How fortunate that those two fighting roosters had trampled my tacos. Otherwise, I would have landed who knows where with food poisoning.

Broken through the Ice

The little town of Wilton is situated in a flat area with no mountains nearby where one could ski in the winter. But fortunately there was a little stream that froze over every cold winter, and the young people could play around on the ice. On one side of the stream the water flowed under the ice in a deeper area. One had to be careful not to get too close to that spot. It was very dangerous. Two brothers experienced what is reported here:

On a January day we town boys were tumbling around on the ice. I was there with my four-year-old brother. I looked after him, but I did not want to have to always be right with him. In one moment that I was not paying enough attention the accident happened. He ran in the direction of the flowing water where the ice became thinner, broke through it, and sank. A scream! The other boys stormed over to the bank and pointed at the hole where my brother had gone down. Without thinking, I ran over to that spot. Then the thought sparked in my mind: 'The flowing water had already carried him further downstream.' I estimated the distance that the current could have carried him, changed direction and ran on the ice further down. With a powerful jump I broke a hole in the ice and went into the water. It was only shoulder deep at this place. By looking down I could see under the water. And there came my brother, carried by the current under the ice!

I grabbed him. He appeared lifeless. I lugged him onto my shoulder. With a very great effort, and constantly breaking through the ice, I was finally able to reach solid ground. Fighting the ice and water had caused me to shake the little one pretty hard, which caused him to vomit out the water he had swallowed. Slowly he came to himself again.

Now I had to get him home as fast as possible. I ran through the streets carrying him on my back. Passersby watched us with surprised looks and shaking heads. I had no time to answer questions. Mother was at home. I quickly explained what had happened. My brother, still a little out of it, was dried off and put into a warm bed. I got dry clothes, and both of us were given hot tea to drink.

What a stroke of fate that I caught my brother exactly at the spot where I broke a hole in the ice. Everything was so hectic and frantic that it was only afterward I had the feeling that someone had been shouting directions in my head.

On the Niesen Mountain

*T*he north face of the Niesen Alp is very steep. In spring one hears the thundering sound of avalanches and rock slides. But, also in spring, the mountain becomes very attractive to people because rare alpine flowers can be found there. Younger people often think little of the danger when the mountain is standing there so silently. But it only takes one deer running through the soft snow high above to unleash an avalanche. Two close friends experienced something like that. Hans, the oldest, told me this story:

It was spring. My classmates and I were just about to graduate. One Sunday we hiked together in the direction of the Niesen. On the upper part of the mountain there was still a lot of snow, but down below it was beginning to turn green. I knew that now in the crevices the first golden yellow auricula would be blooming.

There is an unwritten rule that before the last avalanche has come down in the spring, one should not climb the north face of the mountain. But as we were strolling around the foot of the impressive mountain and looking up at the majestic peak, we agreed to climb up a little way and look for the alpine flower. We climbed along the edge of an avalanche path that had already started to green. On some of the pine trees we could read the signs of destruction from earlier avalanches. Suddenly, from high above—a faraway thundering! Lightning quick something told me: "Grab onto a tree!" Already the avalanche was crashing down. My friend was caught up by the air pressure, flew through the air, and landed further down in some low bushes.

When the roaring stopped and the shower of rocks was quiet, I released my arms from the tree. Stillness like a grave surrounded me. A cry sounded from below: "Hans, where are you?" I climbed down over snow, debris, and rocks. My friend had rolled from the bushes into rocky rubble and was lying there. His Sunday clothes were torn and ragged, his face and hands bloodied. I helped him up. He could hobble, so nothing was broken! I dabbed with my handkerchief at the blood seeping from his scrapes, but I could not wipe away his bruises. The crevice flowers above in the cliffs remained untouched, no human hand to pick them. I supported my friend so the walk home would go better. We did not say one word. We were probably both thinking the same thing: We could be dead.

I accompanied my friend to his parents' house to try and soothe his father's certain anger. He had a temper and we did not know what would happen. "I'll go ahead!" I said as we got closer to the house. The house door was also the kitchen door. I climbed the steps and knocked. His mother opened the door. His father was sitting at the kitchen table. I was stuttering a little when I said: "We were in an avalanche on the Niesen." "Where is Kari? Has something happened to him?" his mother cried in shock. His father paled and stood up. He looked at me with a horror-stricken expression. I slowly replied: "He's washing the blood off his face down at the hydrant." "Thank God, he's alive!" his mother cried with relief, and both parents hurried down the steps. I waited where I was. His father returned carrying his son in his strong arms, with tears in his eyes. I stayed until Kari had been cared for, bandaged, and put to bed. Later, as I was saying goodbye, Kari whispered: "Today, for the first time, my father showed me that he loves me."

* * *

It was about fifteen years later. The Second World War was raging in Europe. At the foot of the Niesen Alp the Swiss Army had hidden an ammunition dump. I found myself doing military service guarding the ammunition with a well-trained wolfhound. The dog was trained so that during the night rounds if he caught scent of a person he would tug at my leg instead of barking. Any bark would have given away our position.

51

I held the clever dog on leash. As we were walking the rounds on a dark night, suddenly my four-legged companion signaled with a tug on my pants leg that there was someone nearby. I stood still and took out my revolver. Something moved some distance ahead. I called out: "Who's there?" In answer, a bullet whistled past my ear. I immediately returned fire and let the dog off the leash: "Get him!" But there was nothing. The experienced dog found no trace. I walked cautiously toward the place where I had seen someone in the darkness. My flashlight illuminated a red fleck of blood on the ground. "Search, Waldo, search!" The dog sniffed here and there, but came back without picking up a scent. Who

or what had I fired upon? Where did the blood come from? The mystery remained unsolved for a long time.

* * *

It was summer, two years later. The war was over. I was hiking in that same area and came upon a mountain farmer. He had three boys with him and they were cutting hay in a meadow. He invited me to sit down on a bench in front of the barn. The boys continued their work. As we talked the conversation became a little more personal. He told me that he had eight children to feed with his meager holdings. Nearby he had an old house with a barn, two cows, and some goats. If the winter was severe, then he had to shoot a deer once in a while so that the children had enough to eat. He did not have the money to buy a hunting license.

And then he solved the mystery for me. "It was about two years ago. A game warden shot me in the leg. My wife had to make herb compresses and doctor around on my leg for a long time. But the gamekeeper and his dog didn't catch me. I know something that will take any dog off the scent."

I asked if he would tell his secret. He continued: "Just in case something like that would happen, I rub my shoes all over with garlic. No dog would follow me!" His story was interrupted when two lively girls walked up. They brought a basket and jug filled with bread, cheese, and water—sustenance for the haymakers.

My puzzling adventure had been explained, but I remained silent about it. I also was handed a cup and bread and cheese. The farmer said: "The three youngest are at home with their mother."

I was feeling a little peculiar. What would have happened if my shot had killed this father? Or if, because of me, he had become a murderer? As I thanked him with a handshake and said farewell, it seemed to me that fate had led me to meet this companion in destiny so that I could untie one of life's knots. I have never met him again, but in my mind the certainty lives on that, on that day during the war, a protective hand had held sway over both of us.

THE DANCER

One day I met a woman in a nursing home who radiated sunny friendliness. We started talking. She told me that she had been a celebrated dancer in her younger years but that her career had come to an abrupt halt through a stroke of fate. I asked her to tell me about it. She began:

It was a hard and strict training I went through as a young girl in Leipzig to become an expressionistic dancer. But in the Mary Wigman School of Dance my passion also increased my endurance. Many gave up, but I held on until graduation and waited for my big chance. And it came.

At that time there was a world-renowned dancer named Harald Kreuzberg. He hired me as a dancer for guest appearances throughout North America that was to last four months. Hollywood, which even at that time, in the 1930s, had a fascinating ring to it, was among the cities in which we were to appear. We were supposed to begin travel in November. In July I began with the costume preparation. Friends from Czechoslovakia invited me to Bad Kudowa in Schlesien. I made a detour through Prague to a costume design shop that I knew of, and I told my friends that I was going there. After everything was finished at the shop (how happy I was about the costumes!), I went to the train station in Prague.

When I was already on the train, at the last minute the apprentice to the costume designer suddenly appeared with the news that I had received a telephone call at the shop. I was not to get out at the station in N. as we had agreed, but rather two stations later. A car would pick me up there. The train whistle blew and I was on my way. Everything went as planned.

I felt so happy in the car, to be driving through the Bohemian landscape with my friends. How beautifully my life and my career as a dancer stood before me! We were driving in an open car. It was already getting towards evening. It was marvelous to feel the wind tousling through my hair. Then it happened.

The car started skidding around a curve in the road. It banged into a tree and rolled over. We were thrown down a grassy slope, over here, over there. The car rolled after us. But I was the only one that it rolled over! When I began to regain consciousness, I clearly heard a voice inside me say: 'Now you cannot go to America, but it will be good for you!' I opened my eyes. A big, reddish full moon was in the sky. I lay on the grass. I realized that there were excited people around me. I could understand them but could not speak. Remarkably, I was filled with an indescribable exhilaration. My voice returned. I calmed and comforted my hysterical friends!

What followed was a month of pain and suffering. In the hospital, with many operations, my cuts and bruises and broken bones were more or less put right again. For many weeks I lay quietly in a cast. In answer to my question if I would ever walk again, the doctor shrugged his shoulders and comforted: "We can always hope."

After weeks I slowly learned to walk again, step by step. Months later I was finally able to return to my mother in Leipzig. She told me: "The night of the accident I saw you standing by my bed covered in blood." Then I knew just how deeply bonded I was with my mother. She took care of me with love.

A half year later I was standing on the stage again, a miracle to everyone, especially my doctors. The director of the Wigman School of Dance moved away to a foreign country. So I took over as director. I instructed the dancing teachers as well as the dancers. I was able to dance again myself, but this experience had caused a transformation in me. The happiness and passion that dancing had always awakened in me just never came back. Instead a deep longing began inside of me. I felt a need to do some kind of work that would reach more people. I was able to become a teacher at the Academy of Music in the area of rhythm and music education. What the voice inside of me had promised back then had become a reality in my life: "It will be good for you!" Was it my angel? I am absolutely convinced of it.

Like a Lead Cloak

Mrs. Heber had taken the streetcar home from a particular place in the city at least a hundred times. She told about the following event:

I stood on the sidewalk and waited for the streetcar to arrive on the other side of the street. Here there was a place to sit so I sat down. Once I saw the streetcar coming, I would have enough time to get to the other side of the street.

I saw the streetcar coming from my right. I stood up to cross the street. I started walking quickly. I did not look in the other direction. Suddenly I felt from above me such a pressure, like a cloak of lead was being put over me. I could not move a muscle and had to stand still. At the same moment, from the left side, another streetcar raced past me. I would certainly have been run over. Like lightning, the thought bored into my mind: 'Those are the wings of your guardian angel pressing down on you!'

As soon as the streetcar passed, the pressure was gone. I reached my streetcar on the other side. Everything happened in just seconds. I had never before experienced my guardian in such a physical way.

THE RESCUE

*T*his story comes from a young woman's travel report: A while back I had seen pictures of the Bretagne area with its granite coast where the ocean crashes in, and they awakened in me the desire to travel there. I went on a group tour. We came to the Atlantic Coast. One morning we visited the narrow Quiberon Peninsula. Through the bus window I spied the incredible, jutting cliffs that stuck out into the ocean like raw tongues. 'I have to go there!' I said to myself. We had the afternoon free. I took public transportation back to Quiberon. I hurried to the place I had seen earlier. Fishermen walked toward me. One of them turned to me with the words: "Il monte!" (It rises.) Because it went upward a little, I thought he meant the trail. But instead he was warning me that the tide was coming in. I went out a little ways and sat on a boulder. I admired the foaming ocean waves and enjoyed the music of the thundering roar. Suddenly I noticed that the water was really rising. I could not be seen from the shore. Somewhat anxious, I started to go back. Standing on top of a rock, I could see that the rising tide had already cut me off from shore. At my feet was a wildly gurgling mass of water. I was not skillful enough to swim in this roiling water, and it rose and rose.

In the midst of despair I discovered, still small in the distance, a man was bounding toward the water. He stood still and looked all around. I waved like crazy. He saw me and hurried again, coming towards me! Oh, a person! A rescuer? He finally came to a rock that jutted out fairly close to me and reached out his arm. With the courage of complete desperation, I took the chance and jumped toward him. He caught me and lifted me up. In flying haste we strove toward the land, bounding over swirling, flooding water. I would never have been able to make it by myself. We reached the safe shore and then the street. We had not exchanged one word.

A car was parked there and inside sat a young woman. I greeted her in French and she said: "Right here at this spot my husband suddenly stopped and said: 'I have to go out there!' I begged him not to risk his life in the tide, to think of our little baby that I'm carrying under my heart. But he was already gone, jumping over the rocks toward the ocean." I explained to her that I was in mortal danger and he had rescued me.

He then began to comfort his wife and talk to her in English. He was British and spoke only English. I did not understand a word. I could tell from his tone that he was trying to calm her. I could not even thank him with words. So I did it with a handshake and tears. They offered to take me in their car back to the hotel.

That night it was a full moon and the entire coast of Bretagne was regaled by a powerful, flooding storm. I would have drowned miserably. I have thought about the incident often: Who gave the young man the idea to stop the car right at that spot and hurry to the sea, actually, hurry to me? I sensed that he was meant to be my rescuer.

Over the Precipice

*H*anspeter was like a lone wolf in the mountains. From time to time he liked to wander alone over the alpine meadows and mountains where nobody bothered him with their talk; only nature spoke to him. One time he told the story of this unusual experience in the mountains:

I was still young then and once again alone in the lonely mountains. My only companion was my backpack. I especially liked to go to a precipice and try and overcome my fear and dizziness. If I felt a certain prickling sensation or the beginning of a shiver I thought: 'You're afraid again!' and I would practice standing at the very edge until all my anxiety was gone.

One time I was on the top of a cliff where the wall went down three hundred meters. I walked to the very edge and did not notice that I was standing on a loose rock. When it tipped I lost my balance, made a desperate turning motion, and fell over the edge. The shock caused me to lose my senses. My life passed before my inner eye like a film! How long it lasted, I do not know. When I came to myself again I was hanging in the air. What had happened? The straps of my backpack had caught on a broken-off trunk of a scrub pine. Beneath me was the abyss. After this shock it took a little while hanging there to realize what my situation was. I was young and strong and was able to right myself onto the tree trunk. With concentration I began to pull myself up, finding footholds on the cliff wall. The tree held. I was able to loosen the straps. As an experienced climber I determinedly climbed back up the approximately ten meters that I had fallen. Once I was back at the top I hugged my backpack and pressed my face to it. My whole body was shaking. There is such a thing as prayer without words! After I had calmed down, a feeling of pure joy coursed through me. *You can live! You can live again!*

I began my descent into the valley. I greeted the trees, the clouds, and the bubbling brook. After that my life changed quite drastically; after many years I started reading the New Testament in the Bible again.

On the Glacier

There are certain experiences that a person never forgets, that give one new confidence in life. I was standing in front of a mountain hut with my hiking partner, looking at the crystal clear starry sky. We were trying to identify the constellations: Virgo, Leo, Big Dipper, Cassiopeia!

In the early morning we had climbed to a high peak. The flushing colors of the sunrise accompanied us. Later, during the descent, we would be able to loosen the safety ropes that had been useful to us on the way up.

Next to the steep glacier, on a lateral moraine, there was a good path without ice. One time I stood still to look at the incredible ice tower formations looming over deep fissures in the glacier. I longed to go climb one of those ice towers from the back side. It would require only a short detour. "As you like," my friend said. "I will follow you."

We put our backpacks and rope on the ground. I led the way over the ascending sheet of ice that was covered with hard, frozen snow. Up ahead I came to the icy edge of a wild, deep fissure. Without thinking of the danger, I trudged on to my goal, the top of the ice tower. My friend followed me with careful steps about twenty meters behind. Now I was up there and looked down at the bizarre cracks and fissures with deep shimmering blue between them. I did not register what the quiet whirring sound was. Then suddenly, from inside me, a powerful voice cried: "Get back!" Immediately I jumped back two, three steps, I don't know how. Before me the entire dome of the ice tower thundered into the deep, right at the place where I had been standing. I stood there as if nailed to the snow. My friend, who was pale from shock, trotted up to me and reached out his hand: "Come on, we have to get out of here!" I tried to lift a leg. I couldn't. My feet were like lead. It took a few minutes for the paralysis to subside. I could walk again. I knew that I had not taken those huge jumps backwards on my own. Something had taken over my legs, something that decided between life and death. But now my own will had returned to me.

After we arrived back at the place where we had left our backpacks and rope, I glanced up at the ice tower I had climbed. It was just a stump now. The many cubic meters of ice had roared into the abyss. My hiking partner and I had never been as silent as we were on the hike back to the valley. Each word would have diminished the impact of the experience.

In one of the nights following the event I had a dream. I was on a sled with my friend and we were riding from the top of a mountain down to the valley. We were swishing along nicely. From below a light shone. A figure walked out of the light and held up his hand in greeting. It was as if he were saying: "Forward! Keep going!" Then I woke up.